J B Castro
Wheeler, Jill C.,
Fidel Castro : Cuban revolutionary
 leader /
$32.79

# FIDEL CASTRO
## CUBAN REVOLUTIONARY LEADER

BY JILL C. WHEELER

**CONTENT CONSULTANT**
Aviva Chomsky
Professor of History
Salem State University

**Core Library**

An Imprint of Abdo Publishing
abdopublishing.com

Cover image: Fidel Castro led the island nation of Cuba for nearly 50 years.

**abdopublishing.com**

Published by Abdo Publishing, a division of ABDO, PO Box 398166, Minneapolis, Minnesota 55439. Copyright © 2018 by Abdo Consulting Group, Inc. International copyrights reserved in all countries. No part of this book may be reproduced in any form without written permission from the publisher. Core Library™ is a trademark and logo of Abdo Publishing.

Printed in the United States of America, North Mankato, Minnesota
042017
092017

Cover Photo: Javier Galeano/AP Images
Interior Photos: Javier Galeano/AP Images, 1; picture-alliance/dpa/AP Images, 4–5, 45; Tor Eigeland/Rex Features/AP Images, 7; J. Marshall/Tribaleye Images/Alamy, 10–11; Ben Martin/The LIFE Images Collection/Getty Images, 13; Diario De La Marina/AP Images, 14; Files/AFP/Getty Images, 18–19; Zuma Press, Inc./Alamy, 21; Shutterstock Images, 23; AP Images, 24, 28; Grey Villet/The LIFE Picture Collection/Getty Images, 26–27; Miguel Vinas/AFP/Getty Images, 31; Charles Tasnadi/AP Images, 34–35, 39 (Castro); White House, 39 (Eisenhower), 39 (Johnson), 39 (Clinton); Cecil Stoughton/White House Photographs/National Archives, 39 (Kennedy); Department of Defense/Department of the Army/National Archives, 39 (Nixon), 39 (Ford), 39 (Carter); US Government, 39 (Reagan), 39 (H.W. Bush); Eric Draper/White House/Department of Defense, 39 (W. Bush)

Editor: Heidi Schoof
Imprint Designer: Maggie Villaume
Series Design Direction: Maggie Villaume

**Publisher's Cataloging-in-Publication Data**

Names: Wheeler, Jill C., author.
Title: Fidel Castro : Cuban revolutionary leader / by Jill C. Wheeler.
Other titles: Cuban revolutionary leader
Description: Minneapolis, MN : Abdo Publishing, 2018. | Series: Newsmakers | Includes bibliographical references and index.
Identifiers: LCCN 2017930439| ISBN 9781532111808 (lib. bdg.) | ISBN 9781680789652 (ebook)
Subjects: LCSH: Castro, Fidel, 1926-2016 --Juvenile literature. | Cuba--History--1959-1990--Juvenile literature. | Heads of state--Cuba--Biography--Juvenile literature. | Revolutionaries--Cuba--Biography--Juvenile literature.
Classification: DDC 972.9106 [B]--dc23
LC record available at http://lccn.loc.gov/2017930439

# CONTENTS

# A HERO RETURNS

The streets of Havana, Cuba, hummed with energy. It was January 8, 1959. On January 1, the country's dictator had fled Cuba. His name was Fulgencio Batista. Batista's critics said he only helped rich Cubans. They said he did nothing to help the poor. Now thousands of Cubans had gathered. They wanted to see the rebel leader who had pushed Batista out of power. He was a tall, bearded, 32-year-old man named Fidel Castro.

Castro and his followers already had held rallies in several other Cuban cities. Now they moved toward Havana, the capital.

Fidel Castro, *center*, and other revolutionaries celebrate their victory over Cuban dictator Fulgencio Batista in 1959.

Castro rode into Havana in a jeep. He was dressed in military clothing. He made his way to a rally at Camp Columbia. This had been Batista's headquarters. Castro stepped up to a podium. He began to address the cheering crowd.

## BATISTA'S CUBA

Fulgencio Batista served as president of Cuba from 1940 to 1944. He ruled as dictator from 1952 to 1959. Batista favored wealthy Cubans over the working class. He oversaw the growth of Havana and built his own private fortune. He took away rights Cubans had come to expect under their constitution.

When Cubans began to rebel, Batista ordered the police to kill his opponents. He lost the support of the US government in 1958. He left Cuba and lived the rest of his life in exile.

Castro did not have a prepared speech. He did not have any notes. He spoke with passion until dawn. Then someone released a flock of white doves. The doves symbolized a new era of peace. One landed on Castro's shoulder. The crowd went wild. They began chanting his name. Many believed the

Fidel Castro was known for giving very long speeches. His victory speech in Havana lasted until morning.

dove was a special sign. They believed it represented Castro's role as savior of their nation.

## CREATING A LEGEND

Castro also believed he was his country's savior. His journey to Havana had started years before. He led a rebel attack on the government in 1953. The attack failed. Castro was arrested, tried, sentenced, and then released. He sought exile in Mexico and returned to Cuba in 1956. Upon his return, he and his followers began a campaign of guerrilla warfare. They operated out of the rugged Sierra Maestra mountains on Cuba's south coast. An army ambush nearly wiped out the rebels just three days after landing. However, the 16 survivors regrouped. They successfully attacked a small garrison on January 17, 1957.

At the same time, another rebel group was weakening Batista's control. The Revolutionary Directorate oversaw a series of bombings. They also encouraged strikes by workers. The group attacked the presidential palace in March 1957. Its leader was a student named José Antonio Echeverría.

## THE *NEW YORK TIMES*

The *New York Times* played a major role in introducing the world to Fidel Castro. Castro's supporters contacted the newspaper in 1957 to have their leader interviewed. *Times* reporter Herbert L. Matthews disguised himself to gain access to where Castro was hiding.

Matthews wrote three articles about Castro. The first was published in February 1957. Matthews called Castro an educated man of ideals, courage, and leadership ability. His articles repeated Castro's claims that he did not want Cuba to become a communist nation.

Army soldiers killed Echeverría following the palace attack. Like Castro, Echeverría was a popular leader and public speaker.

Many historians believe Echeverría's death cleared the way for Castro. It allowed him to take control of the revolution. Castro had captured the hearts of Cubans. He was already a legend by the time he arrived in Havana. His popularity among the Cuban people made it possible for him to quickly control the nation.

## EXPLORE ONLINE

Chapter One focuses on Castro's popularity. His supporters often used colorful posters to promote Castro and his ideas. The website below shows some of these images. As you know, every source is different. What are the similarities between Chapter One and the information you found on the website? Are there any differences? How do the two sources present information differently?

*NEW YORK TIMES:* CASTRO'S REVOLUTION, ILLUSTRATED
abdocorelibrary.com/fidel-castro

# ROUGH-AND-TUMBLE CHILDHOOD

Fidel Alejandro Castro Ruz was born August 13, 1926. Some reports say he was born in 1927. His parents lived near Birán in the Oriente province of eastern Cuba. His father was Ángel Castro y Argiz. Ángel was a plantation owner. He had moved to Cuba from Spain.

Fidel was the fifth of nine children. Ángel had two children by his first wife, a schoolteacher named María Argota. He then had seven children with a woman named Lina Ruz González. Lina was a maid in the

Four-year-old Fidel posed for a formal portrait on his father's estate around 1930.

## FROM SPAIN TO CUBA

Ángel Castro was born in one of Spain's poorest regions. He was drafted to fight for Spain in the Cuban War of Independence. The United States declared war on Spain in 1898. US forces won the war and pushed Spain out of Cuba.

Ángel left Cuba following Spain's defeat. He later returned to Cuba to find work. He began by selling lemonade. He also worked on a railroad. Later he bought a lumber mill. Eventually he began doing business with the American-owned United Fruit Company. Ángel Castro controlled some 25,000 acres (10,117 ha) of land by the time Fidel was born.

Castro household. Ángel married Lina many years after Fidel was born.

## FIDEL'S EARLY LIFE

Fidel began his education at age three. He started out in the one-room school on his father's estate. But he often did not behave. He would throw tantrums if he did not get his way. Sometimes he would yell at the teacher and run home.

At age six, his father sent him to live with a teacher. He lasted there a year and a half. Next he was sent to

Fidel, a natural athlete, played baseball throughout his life.

a boarding school. Fidel continued to make trouble. He often fought with his teachers and classmates. He wanted to be first in everything. When he did not win, he was a poor loser.

## STUDENT AND ATHLETE

Fidel was nine when his parents sent him to the Colegio de Dolores prep school. But Fidel was not a typical student. He was from the country. He was used to the

rough language and habits of workers. His classmates looked down on him. Fidel responded by gaining their respect in sports. He showed special talent for baseball and soccer.

In sports Fidel could impress his wealthy classmates. But he had another gift. Fidel had a photographic memory. He could quote whole textbook pages from memory. This allowed him to succeed in the classroom as well as on the playing field.

Fidel attended high school at the elite Colegio de Belén in Havana. The school was the best in the country. Jesuits ran the school. Fidel had to wear a uniform and attend church. The school emphasized Spanish culture and ideas. Fidel's favorite subjects were history and debating. He especially enjoyed military history. He also liked talking in public. He loved trying to win people over to his point of view.

The caption for Fidel's 1945 high school yearbook photo reads: "Distinguished student and a fine athlete. Very popular. Will study law and we have no doubt he will have a brilliant future."

# LAW STUDENT AND ACTIVIST

Fidel graduated from high school in 1945. He then entered law school at the University of Havana. Before college, Fidel had little interest in politics. That quickly changed. The university was caught up in student activism. Students were talking of a Cuba free of American influence. They spoke about the rights of workers. They questioned the privileges given to land and factory owners.

Fidel became involved. He led student protests. Fidel found school to be easy. He did not need to study. He only had to memorize things. The young Fidel spent his time in political meetings.

In the summer of 1947, Fidel joined with other rebels from Cuba, the Dominican Republic, Venezuela, and Costa Rica. They trained to help overthrow Dominican dictator Rafael Trujillo. The mission failed. Still, the experience gave Fidel a taste for military operations. He followed that expedition with trips to

Venezuela, Panama, and Colombia. In Colombia he participated in anti-government protests and took weapons from the local police.

Fidel graduated with his law degree in 1949. He began working to help poor Cubans. It was hard to pay the bills that way. Sometimes his clients did not have money to pay him. By 1952 he had abandoned his work as an attorney. He turned his attention to politics.

## MARRIAGE AND CHILDREN

Fidel married Mirta Díaz-Balart in October 1948, while he was at the university. The Díaz-Balarts were wealthy. They were close to the family of Fulgencio Batista. Batista even gave the couple $1,000 as a wedding gift.

Fidel and Mirta had one son, Fidel Ángel. They called him Fidelito. He was born September 1, 1949. The marriage did not last. Fidel was at political meetings more than he was home. His wife never knew whether they would be able to pay the rent. The couple divorced in December 1954, while Fidel was in prison. Fidel later had six more children with longtime companion Dalia Soto del Valle.

# FROM EXILE TO VICTORY

At that time, a corrupt president named Carlos Prío Socarrás ran Cuba. Castro ran for the Cuban Congress in 1952. But the election never took place. General Fulgencio Batista staged a coup. Then he set himself up as dictator. The United States supported Batista. Wealthy Cubans supported him as well.

Castro disliked the Batista government. He began making plans to overthrow it. He had many followers by this time. On July 26, 1953,

In 1953 Castro, *center*, and his supporters planned and carried out an attack on the Moncada Barracks in Santiago de Cuba.

he and his supporters attacked a military base. The attack failed. Many of the attackers were killed.

Castro and his brother Raúl were captured and put on trial. Castro defended himself in court. He gave a speech telling why he wanted to overthrow the government. He ended the speech by saying he did not fear prison. He said history would clear his name.

The court convicted Castro. The judge sentenced him to 15 years in jail. But the government released Castro and the other rebels early. They were freed in May 1955, after just two years in jail.

## THE ROOTS OF REBELLION

Cuba in the 1940s and 1950s was a playground for the rich and famous. The island's sunshine and casinos drew visitors from around the world. Organized crime groups worked with the Cuban government to build casinos. Then they took a share of the profits. But the projects were funded in part with public money. That money was meant for Cuban development and retirement funds. Many workers remained poor and landless.

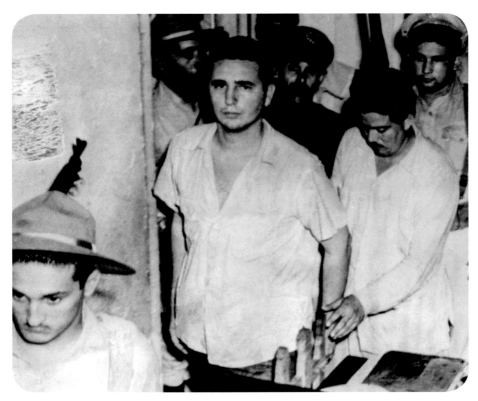

Castro and other survivors of the failed attack returned to their revolutionary ways as soon as they were released from prison.

## EXILED

Castro and his brother fled to Mexico. Mexico offered political asylum to revolutionaries. They found many other Cubans living there. Most of them opposed the Cuban government. They also met revolutionaries from other countries throughout Latin America. One of them was Argentine rebel Che Guevara.

The group of exiles often gathered to discuss politics. They shared ideas about how to improve the lives of poor people. They debated what could be done to change things. They believed the only way was to overthrow the existing government. They would start their revolution in Cuba through guerrilla warfare.

Their campaign began in late 1956. Castro and about 80 others boarded an old wooden yacht. They packed it with weapons and set sail for Cuba. The group hoped to arrive in time to support another

## CHE GUEVARA

**Castro met an Argentine doctor named Ernesto "Che" Guevara while he was in exile. The two became close friends. They shared many of the same ideas. Guevara held several positions in the Cuban government after Castro came to power. He was put in charge of Cuba's Revolutionary Tribunals. They were used to try, convict, and execute pro-Batista political prisoners. He also worked on land reform and literacy initiatives. Guevara left Cuba in 1965. He worked to start a revolution in Bolivia. The Bolivian Army captured and killed him in 1967.**

# CASTRO'S CUBA

Castro grew up on the Eastern side of the island of Cuba. This also was where he based his guerrilla campaign. This map shows the location of places that played a major role in Cuban history during Castro's life.

planned rebellion. But the heavily loaded boat and poor weather delayed them. They ended up stuck in the mud. They waded ashore to Cuba on December 2.

In Cuba Castro and the others organized citizens who believed in their cause. They created groups of supporters in cities and small towns. Castro even created his own government in some areas. It operated at the same time as the Batista government. Castro's government focused on improving the lives of peasants. At the same time, he and his supporters engaged in

Batista's army was unable to suppress Castro and his guerrilla rebels.

military campaigns. They wanted to take key parts of the country by force.

Batista started to worry about Castro and his rebellion. He ordered Cuban troops to kill Castro if they could. The army often reported that it had done so. Then the report would turn out to be false. Castro became more popular with each military victory.

# STRAIGHT TO THE
# SOURCE

During his trial, Castro acted as his own lawyer. He gave a long speech defending his group's fight against the corrupt Batista government. He later wrote it down from memory. These were his closing words:

> I come to the close of my defense plea but I will not end it as lawyers usually do, asking that the accused be freed. I cannot ask freedom for myself while my comrades are already suffering. . . . It is understandable that honest men should be dead or in prison in a Republic where the President is a criminal and a thief. . . . I know that imprisonment will be harder for me than it has ever been for anyone. . . . But I do not fear prison, as I do not fear the fury of the miserable tyrant who took the lives of 70 of my comrades. Condemn me. It does not matter. History will absolve me.

> Source: Fidel Castro. "History Will Absolve Me." *Castro Internet Archive*. Marxists.org, 2001. Web. Accessed January 2, 2017.

## What's the Big Idea?

Take a close look at this passage. Why does Castro feel justified in trying to overthrow the government? Pick out two details he uses to make his point. What are some words he uses to describe President Batista?

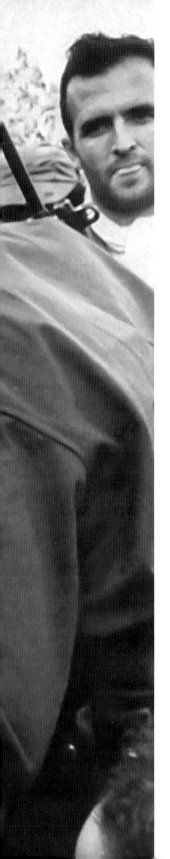

# TAKING CONTROL

D ecember 1958 marked two full years of guerrilla war by Castro and other rebels. On New Year's Eve 1958, Castro was preparing to attack Santiago de Cuba. Guevara had just declared victory around the central Cuban city of Santa Clara. Raúl Castro was about to take control of Guantanamo. Batista was collecting cash and close friends. He prepared to leave the country. He departed just after midnight.

Castro and his rebels made their way toward Havana. People cheered and celebrated as they passed through cities and villages. On January 8, 1959, Castro

Castro was a hero to many Cubans who had suffered under Batista's rule.

entered the capital. He gave his victory speech at Camp Columbia.

Castro moved quickly to break up the remains of the Batista government. The rebel leaders formed a new government. Castro was the commander in chief of the military. In February the new prime minister resigned. Castro took his place. In tribunals, the rebels arrested, tried, and killed more than 500 Batista supporters.

Castro had often said he was not a communist. Those statements became harder to believe. By late 1959, Cuba's government took control of the economy. Castro also moved to silence any news media who were critical of him. Castro was successful in improving education and health care for many Cubans. However, he took away their freedom of speech. Wealthy Cubans found they had fewer economic opportunities. Poor Cubans suddenly had more. US leaders viewed the

Former Cuban president and dictator Fulgencio Batista spent the rest of his life in exile. He died in Spain in 1973.

events in Cuba with concern. By late 1959, they began making plans to oust the revolutionaries.

## MIXED RESULTS

Many Cuban professionals, including engineers, doctors, and lawyers, disagreed with Castro. They began to leave Cuba for the United States. This led to economic problems for Cuba. More than one million Cuban exiles moved to the United States.

Meanwhile, lower-class Cubans benefited from Castro's policies. Many more Cubans learned to read and write. In addition, the Cuban people received better health care than they had before.

## SOVIET TIES

The United States broke off diplomatic relations with Cuba in January 1961. In April of that year, US-trained Cuban exiles began a military action against Cuba. It became known as the Bay of Pigs invasion. The goal of the invasion was to remove Castro from power. Cuban exiles flying American planes set out to destroy Castro's air force. But Castro had learned of the invasion in

Many of the Bay of Pigs invaders were taken prisoner by Castro's troops.

advance, so he had moved his forces. The air strike was followed by a ground invasion on Cuba's remote southern coast. Castro's forces were waiting. Most of the 1,200 invaders were killed or captured.

In October 1962, Castro and Soviet leader Nikita Khrushchev agreed to put Soviet nuclear missiles in Cuba. Castro wanted to defend against the possibility of another US-backed invasion. An American spy plane discovered the plan. President John F. Kennedy demanded that the missiles be removed.

## BRINKMANSHIP

Kennedy sought to show that the United States would not back down. His tough stance during the missile crisis is an example of what is known as *brinkmanship*. It refers to the practice of winning a confrontation by pushing events to the brink of active conflict.

On October 22, he announced the United States would put a blockade around Cuba. This would prevent any more weapons from reaching the island.

The next 13 days saw a series of

tense discussions. US and Soviet leaders reached an agreement at last. The United States agreed not to invade Cuba. The Soviets agreed to remove the missiles from Cuba. In exchange the United States also agreed to remove missiles it had placed in Turkey.

## FURTHER EVIDENCE

Chapter Four talks about the Cuban Missile Crisis. Visit the website below. Can you find information that details Cuba's role during the crisis? What was the impact of the crisis on the relationship between the United States and the Soviet Union?

**NATIONAL PUBLIC RADIO: CUBAN MISSILE CRISIS**
abdocorelibrary.com/fidel-castro

# LEADING CUBA

Cuba continued to be a concern for US officials. In February 1963, President Kennedy banned US citizens from traveling there. Trade with Cuba was blocked. This took a major toll on Cuba's economy. Castro continued to round up people who opposed him. The Cuban government sentenced them to prison or forced labor. Castro harassed local clergy. Many closed their churches. He created a program to get people to spy on their own neighbors. His policies made life difficult for many Cubans.

At the same time, Cubans had won a historic revolution. Cuba was just a small island, yet it was known globally. People around

The beard, military fatigues, and cap were all part of Castro's popular image.

the world looked to Cuba as an example of what could happen when poor people united. Cubans had improved access to health care, education, and housing, making Castro widely popular. Activists in other nations were inspired to seek their fair share. Castro also worked to spread his revolution to other countries.

In the 1970s, an investigation revealed that the US government had tried to kill Castro. It had tried on eight different occasions between 1960 and 1965. Castro was aware of many of the attempts. He liked to boast about how many times he had escaped death. Meanwhile, Castro forged even tighter ties with the Soviet Union. Many Soviet engineers, technicians, and soldiers found new homes in Cuba.

US-Cuban relations thawed briefly beginning in March 1977 during the administration of US president Jimmy Carter. Cuban Americans were allowed to visit relatives in Cuba. Relations took a turn for the worse in 1980. Discontent in Cuba had forced Castro to permit the Mariel Boatlift. Many Cubans were allowed to leave the country. The event caused then-president Ronald Reagan to re-establish the travel ban in 1982.

## DEFIANT TO THE END

In 1999 the US Coast Guard found a young Cuban boy floating in an inner tube near Florida. His name was Elián González. Elián, his mother, and 12 others had been trying to escape to the United States. Their small boat sank, and the boy's mother drowned. Elián was put in the custody of family members in Miami, Florida. Castro stepped in to get the boy returned to his father in Cuba.

## THE MARIEL BOATLIFT

Many Cubans fled the country when Castro came to power. Many others wanted to escape as the years of Castro's rule stretched on. In 1980 Castro tried to make the Cuban people happier by letting some leave. The Mariel Boatlift was named after the beach from which 125,000 Cubans left their country for Florida. They left in boats, flimsy rafts, and even inner tubes.

## TROUBLED ECONOMY

Before Castro took over, the United States had been a major trading partner for Cuba. Beginning in the 1960s, US leaders tried to weaken the Cuban economy enough to force Castro out of power. Cuba turned to the Soviet Union. The Soviets bought Cuban sugar and helped the nation's economy.

Castro found himself on his own again in 1991. The Soviet Union collapsed. The Cuban economy began to slow down. Castro realized he had to do things differently than in the past. In 1993 he made it legal for Cubans to use American dollars sent from family members outside of Cuba. He also opened up the country to foreign investment and tourism.

Castro celebrated 40 years in power in 1999. Many Cubans had never known any other leader. In 2001 Castro appeared to faint while giving a speech. In 2004 he was stepping off a platform when he stumbled and fell. The signs of aging encouraged his opponents. One of them spread a petition demanding reforms, including free speech.

An official statement in July 2006 said Castro had undergone surgery.

# OUTLASTING THE
# PRESIDENTS

US presidents are limited to two terms of four years each. Castro ruled Cuba during the administrations of 11 different US presidents. What are the advantages of term limits? What are the disadvantages?

 Dwight D. Eisenhower (1953–1961)

 John F. Kennedy (1961–1963)

 Lyndon B. Johnson (1963–1969)

 Richard Nixon (1969–1974)

 Gerald Ford (1974–1977)

 Jimmy Carter (1977–1981)

 Ronald Reagan (1981–1989)

 George H.W. Bush (1989–1993)

 Bill Clinton (1993–2001)

 George W. Bush (2001–2009)

 1959

2008

**Fidel Castro (1959–2008)**

The statement said he was temporarily giving power to his younger brother Raúl. In 2008 Castro resigned due to age and failing health. The change in power led to other changes as well. In 2009 President Barack Obama lifted the restrictions on US citizens visiting family members in Cuba and sending them money. He also allowed Americans to take trips to Cuba. In March 2016, Obama became the first sitting US president to meet with a Cuban leader in 85 years.

Castro died in Havana on November 25, 2016, at the age of 90. For the people who suffered under his rule and for those who escaped from Cuba, he is remembered as a brutal dictator. To others, including many Cubans, he remains a hero who improved Cubans' lives and brought hope to oppressed peoples around the world.

# STRAIGHT TO THE
# SOURCE

As Castro aged, some of his opponents stepped up their calls for change. This passage from Castro's obituary in the *New York Times* details one of those initiatives.

*As Mr. Castro and his revolution aged, Cuban dissidents grew bolder. Oswaldo Payá, using a clause in the Cuban Constitution, collected thousands of signatures in a petition demanding a referendum on free speech and other political freedoms. (Mr. Payá died in a car crash in 2012.) Bloggers wrote disparagingly of Mr. Castro and the regime, although most of their missives could not be read in Cuba, where internet access was strictly limited.*

Source: Anthony DePalma. "Fidel Castro, Cuban Revolutionary Who Defied U.S., Dies at 90." *New York Times*. New York Times, November 26, 2016. Web. Accessed April 28, 2017.

## Point of View

This passage was published after Castro's death in a US newspaper. What views does this passage reflect? How do you think this would change had it appeared in a Cuban newspaper after Castro's death?

# IMPORTANT
# DATES

**1926**
Fidel Alejandro Castro Ruz is born on his family's sugar plantation in Birán, Cuba, on August 13.

**1945**
Castro attends the University of Havana Law School.

**1948**
Castro marries Mirta Díaz-Balart on October 12; the couple divorce in 1954.

**1953**
Castro organizes a rebellion that attacks the Moncada Barracks near Santiago on July 26; the revolt is unsuccessful, and Castro is arrested and sentenced to 15 years in prison.

**1956**
Castro returns to Cuba and creates a stronghold in the Sierra Maestra mountains; his revolutionary movement grows in popularity.

**1959**
Batista flees Cuba on January 1, as Castro's forces enter Havana; Castro assumes the post of commander in chief of the armed forces and later becomes prime minister.

**1961**
Castro's forces fight off a small army of Cuban exiles
in the Bay of Pigs invasion in April.

**1962**
In October, after tense negotiations with the United States,
the Soviet Union agrees to withdraw missiles from Cuba; in
return, the United States agrees not to invade Cuba.

**1977**
Cuban Americans are temporarily allowed to visit relatives
in Cuba.

**1980**
The Mariel Boatlift allows some 125,000 Cubans to leave the
country for the United States.

**1999**
Castro becomes involved in the Elián González affair.
González is eventually returned to his father in Havana.

**2016**
Castro dies in Havana on November 25 at the age
of 90.

# STOP AND THINK

### Dig Deeper

Chapters Four and Five outline Castro's unfriendly relationship with the United States. Yet it was not always that way. Ask an adult to help you find a reliable source of historical information. When did the US government change its mind about Cuba? Why?

### Surprise Me

Chapter Two explores what Fidel Castro was like as a child and teenager. After learning more about him, what things surprised you the most? Write a few sentences about Castro's hobbies, behaviors, and background that seem most unusual based on his role in history.

### Take a Stand

Some Cubans were better off after Castro came to power than they were before. The lower class had better health care and education. Yet many freedoms such as press freedom and freedom of speech were taken away. Was Castro's leadership a good thing for Cuba or was it a bad thing?

## You Are There

This book discusses US travel restrictions to Cuba. People traveling from America were unable to go to Cuba from the early 1960s until travel restrictions were eased in 2016. Imagine that you wished to visit family in Cuba during this period. How do you think you might feel about the travel restriction? Would your feelings depend on how you thought about Castro?

# GLOSSARY

**asylum**
protection from arrest
or harm

**communist**
a person who believes
in a system in which the
government controls all land
and products and there is no
privately owned property

**coup**
a sudden and often violent
attempt by a small group
of people to take over
the government

**dictator**
a person who rules a country
with total authority and often
in a cruel or brutal way

**exile**
a person who has chosen
or been forced to live in a
country that is not his or
her home

**garrison**
troops stationed at a military
camp, fort, or base

**guerrilla**
a soldier who does not
belong to a regular army
and who fights the enemy
through small-scale attacks

**Jesuit**
a member of a Roman
Catholic brotherhood
dedicated to mission work
and education

# LEARN MORE

## Books

George, Enzo. *The Cold War.* New York: Cavendish Square Publishing, 2016.

Hamen, Susan E. *The Cuban Missile Crisis through the Eyes of John F. Kennedy.* Minneapolis, MN: Abdo Publishing, 2016.

Murray, Julie. *Cuba.* Minneapolis, MN: Abdo Publishing, 2014.

## Websites

To learn more about Newsmakers, visit **abdobooklinks.com**. These links are routinely monitored and updated to provide the most current information available.

Visit **abdocorelibrary.com** for free additional tools for teachers and students.

# INDEX

## About the Author

Jill C. Wheeler is the author of nearly 300 nonfiction books for young readers, covering everything from science and environmental topics to biographies of celebrities. Wheeler lives in Minneapolis, Minnesota, with her husband and whichever of their three adult daughters happens to be visiting at the time.